It Pays to Praise

IT PAY$ TO *praise*

Sharon F. Marks

Miles River Press

1009 Duke Street
Alexandria, Virginia 22314
(800) 767-1501 (703) 683-1500

PUBLISHED BY:
  MILES RIVER PRESS
  1009 Duke Street
  Alexandria, Virginia 22314

PUBLISHING TEAM
Peg Paul, Publisher
Betty Katz, Editor
Libby Schroeder, Marketing Coordinator
Bill Raue, Cover Design
Susan Bliss Nealon, Design and Production

ORDERING INFORMATION
Orders by individuals and organizations. Miles River Press publications are available through bookstores or can be ordered direct from the publisher at the Miles River Press address or by calling 1 (800) 767-1501.

QUANTITY SALES. Miles River Press publications are available at special quantity discounts when purchased in bulk by corporations, associations, and others. For details, write to Special Sales Department at the Miles River Press address or call (703) 683-1500.

ORDERS BY U.S. TRADE BOOKSTORES AND WHOLESALERS. Contact Atrium Publishers Group, 3356 Coffey Lane, Santa Rosa, CA 954023; tel (707)542-5400; fax (707)542-5444.

ORDERS FOR COLLEGE COURSE ADOPTION USE. Contact Miles River Press, 1009 Duke Street, Alexandria, VA 22314; tel (703)683-1500; fax (703) 683-0827.

LIBRARY OF CONGRESS CATALOGING-IN-PUBLICATION DATA:
  Marks, Sharon F., 1944-
  It pays to praise / Sharon F. Marks
        p.   cm. — (A self-guided workshop ; 1)
  ISBN 0-917917-07-3 (pbk.)
  1. Psychology, Industrial.   2. Praise   3. Interpersonal communication.
  I. Title   II. Series.
  HF5548.8.M365   1996
  158.7—dc20   95-38646
  Copyright © 1996 by Sharon F. Marks   CIP

10 9 8 7 6 5 4 3 2

TO

Dan Toth who encouraged me to

write this book; Janet Farrar and

Nena Montgomery who helped bring

this book to life; Kim Tarman and

Robin Raber-Luna who practice

praising; and Stan Kurz, who has

consistently and generously helped

me recognize the value of my

own efforts.

TABLE OF CONTENTS

SECTION ONE

"I can live for two months on a good compliment."
— Mark Twain

SECTION TWO

"People only see what they are prepared to see."
— Ralph Waldo Emerson

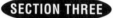

SECTION THREE

"It is much easier to be critical than be correct."
— Benjamin Disraeli

SECTION FOUR

"A company is known by the people it keeps."
— Anonymous

Recognizing effort is what praise is all about. Effort is the essential ingredient that is too often ignored when praise is given. Whether we are at work, at home or in a social situation, it is important to have someone recognize what we try to do. Not only does this acknowledgment "feel good," but when others appreciate our efforts, that recognition contributes to how successful we become do you remember as the focus of the comments you were given?

In today's workplace, employees are constantly challenged to expand their skills and responsibilities. It is vital to acknowledge the daily efforts employees put into learning these skills and assuming new responsibilities. These daily routine efforts link the individual's contribution with the group's overall goal. Without day-to-day effort, organizations would not be able to complete projects, close deals, or meet goals.

Continuing effort is built on a foundation of praise. Whether addressing such diverse areas as planning financial packages, decision making, sharing of information, or supporting noble effort, the praise giver's bottom line is informing employees that others in the organization are aware of their accomplishments. Regardless of the approach used, the praise giver's words must be direct: 'You made a difference, and I am aware of it.' The methods of recognizing praise, however, differ with culture, industry, age, gender, and seniority. Praise givers need to be aware of these differences.

For instance, consider these EXAMPLES:

In France, the absence of variable financial rewards between managers and employees is common.

In Japan, it is believed that the division of quality control should rest 85 percent with workers and 15 percent with management.

In Korea, Kim Woo-Choon, founder of Daewoo, a huge conglomerate involved with a variety of businesses, believes it's important for management to share its knowledge. It is believed that intellectual selfishness is as bad as material selfishness.

And in the United States, at Motorola Inc., they celebrate "noble failure" and believe that an organization demanding constant perfection discourages employees from striving and makes them timid.

The best way to support ongoing effort is with praise — an incredibly powerful tool unlimited in scope, form, and function. Praise giving is not the sole responsibility of one person or of one level in a company. You can make a difference wherever you are in the organization. Letting others know that you are aware of their efforts reinforces the elements essential for business growth — creativity, willingness, and risk taking.

I decided to write a book on praise because, like Gordon Dexter's character in the movie, *'Round Midnight*, "there is not enough kindness in the world." Praise is so easy, so available and has such a terrific end result, how can we not take the time to let others know we appreciate what they are trying to do.

As I worked on this book, I learned that there is little if any information available to help us understand the basis for one's behavior concerning praise. I found no books that offered practical scenarios so skills introduced could actually be practiced. I also was looking for a book that would help people understand that there is a sound business rationale for praising.

It Pays to Praise is the outcome of many hours of listening to people talk about their workplaces, their bosses, colleagues and their own sense of worth. It is my sincere hope that the ideas in this book resonate with the reader on a very personal level, and that people allow themselves the opportunity to both give and receive praise.

Sharon Marks
San Francisco, California
October, 1995

President of Top Marks Consultants, Sharon Marks is a facilitator, consultant, trainer, and strategic planner with over 15 years of experience. She started her own consulting business by providing communications training as the foundation for all other training. Sharon has used this training with information systems clients in the financial industry, research scientists in petroleum industry and personnel divisions of major health care facilities; she also develops strategic plans for newly reorganized divisions within existing companies.

She is also a senior consultant for Project Management Mentors, a San Francisco-based international project management firm, and is a certified master training for Zenger-Miller. She serves as vice president of the San Francisco chapter of the American Society of Training and Development, and is a member of the Innovative Thinking Network, and the International Association of Facilitators.

Before opening her own business she was a senior trainer for Wells Fargo bank where she coordinated, customized and delivered leadership training for a management program involving 25 divisions. Sharon learned the service side of consulting while manager of operations for Decker Communications, Inc.

Sharon Marks would like to hear from you as you develop your own praise techniques. You can reach her through e-mail at:
SHARTSTAN@AOL.COM

On my list of the five most demoralizing and self-defeating Sappers of Spirit and Strength in the Workplace Today, lack of mutual support would rate toward the top. I see all kinds of employees, managers and line staff alike whose behavior betrays how they feel about themselves on the job in all kinds of situations: fear of making creative suggestions in a meeting, unwillingness to offer constructive criticism to co-workers who need feedback, refusal to let anyone know that problems have arisen and there is need of help. Creative and productive potential is being drained from thousands of work hours by insecurity and disconnection with others.

How to offer consistent mutual support in the workplace is among the most needed skills in the American workplace. In this workbook Sharon Marks provides, first, analysis for developing awareness, second, practical suggestions for learning the skills, and third, varied opportunities for personal practice.

Any thoughtful discussion of the methods and technique of praising will raise the broader question of fit in the organizational culture. Why do our workplaces do such a poor job of cultivating mutual support? And why is it so hard for people to praise one another with enthusiasm and sincerity? There are several factors that contribute to our culturally-based discomfort of praising, such as the ever-present fear of taking up too much time. Whatever it may be, I think it's important to be conscious of the true power of praise, for it is an instrument of change; those who praise effectively inevitably become change agents in their work group. Praise penetrates the alientation of our business-as-usual workplace culture to promote relationship and create bonds.

Effective praising, I think, may require more courage, and consciousness, and commitment, than one might expect. And a consistent, responsible effort at praising might pay much higher dividends than one might anticipate, and not only in terms of increased productivity. People might learn to make authentic human connections that come close to the heart on a daily basis.

Sharon Marks is to be commended for her specific and professional approach to humanizing organizational culture. Her book gives opportunities to reflect on the true nature of praise; and it gives us an important set of tools to make the effort, ourselves, to develop and build stronger cultures of mutual support.

Sam Kaner, Ph.D.
Executive Director, Community at Work
San Francisco, California
August, 1995

SECTION ONE

PRAISE

WHAT IS IT?

Praise is a gift gently wrapped in thoughtful words and gracious gestures carefully chosen with the recipient in mind.
—Sharon Marks

KEY POINTS

Praise is defined as an interaction that recognizes and acknowledges effort.

Praise is a flexible, cost-effective tool.

Praise is an essential ingredient in the ongoing daily effort that is the foundation of larger and more visible successes.

Praise is a powerful element in any organization. The results of praise are seen in lower worker turnover, higher production, better quality, retention of key employees, greater communication, and reduced disability claims.

Our life experiences cause us to develop filters that affect our ways of giving and accepting praise.

DEFINING PRAISE

When people ask why "It pays to praise," it's useful to have a common understanding of the term, praise. For the purposes of this workbook, praise is a tool that expresses recognition and approval. Tools are implements that assist with work and make interactions easier, more accessible, productive, and efficient. We use tools to make things happen in ways we see as beneficial and desirable. Tools are implements whose regular use makes effort go well. By that definition, praise is certainly a tool.

The praise tool has multiple functions, formats, and points of focus. It can be something as simple as an e-mail message or a letter in a personnel file. Praise can occur in a formal meeting or by the water cooler; it can come directly from a manager or by way of a colleague.

The emphasis, though, must be on the effort that goes into a project, rather than on the completed project, winning team, or the successful closure of a deal. Sustained effort always precedes success. It's important then to use praise, when employees need encouragement to keep moving.

Praise has the power to transform, to move a person from apathy to action, from stagnation to motivation, and from indecision to decisiveness. This book is designed to encourage you to focus on a wide variety of approaches to praise. It gives you new ideas, helps modify existing ones, and demonstrates how valuable a tool praise is. Think about your own ideas of praise as a tool that recognizes and approves others' efforts.

Consider the following questions and your initial response to each.
What would happen if we were regularly and creatively praised when something went well, rather than criticized when something went wrong?

....

How does your past experience with praise relate to the way you accept praise now?

....

How does the form of praise we give reinforce the receiver's perception of self, team, or organization?

....

Now review the reflections on the next page.

REFLECTIONS

As we begin to think of praise as a tool, let's take a moment to consider just how powerful that tool can be in shaping success. Think also of the flip side of that thought. How can the lack of praise sabotage positive achievement?

- If we were regularly and creatively praised, we would know our individual efforts were being recognized. If the praise were given creatively, it would be seen, felt, and heard as sincere. Because people tend to repeat behavior that is positively reinforced, productivity and quality would continue to increase.

- Past experience influences how we hear praise. For example, if we were raised as perfectionists, believing nothing ever quite measured up, it would be hard to believe any kind of positive recognition we were given. If we rarely heard praise for ourselves, we might not be skilled or comfortable in giving it to others.

- Praise is unlimited in its forms. For example, it can range from a friendly "Thanks for your help!", to a surprise bouquet, to a golf invitation, to a request that we take up a long-sought after position on a project team. The more personalized the praise, the more the receiver knows it is well thought out and carefully considered. Personalized praise lets people know they are recognized as special and unique.

ASSUMPTIONS ABOUT PRAISE
What You Know, What You Think You Know, and What No One Will Tell You

ASSUMPTIONS	REALITY
Money is always appreciated.	In some cultures it is inappropriate to give money as it is thought to cause divisiveness among workers.
Public praise may embarrass someone, but the motivation it provides others is worth it.	For some people, being praised is a private event.
Using a variety of praising methods will cause hurt feelings when someone gets something desired by another.	Praise that is truly valued recognizes that each person makes a distinct contribution.
It's OK to joke when giving praise because the recipient knows what the giver is really trying to say.	Praise is directly linked to the sincerity with which it is offered.
Praise should be given at specific events for specific accomplishments.	Praise is a method to let others know, on a frequent and informal basis, that you are aware and appreciative of their efforts.
If praise is given too frequently, it tends to lose its value.	It's not the frequency but rather the sincerity and individuality that can provide added value.
In today's chaotic workplace, there isn't enough time to praise. Anyway, people should know themselves if what they are doing is right or not.	If there isn't time to praise, is there time to remedy the problems that arise from a lack of praise?

Your ADDITIONS to this list.

....

....

....

....

THE POWER OF PRAISE
Its Impact

Whenever you consider using a new skill, the obvious question is, What are the benefits of using this skill? Praise that is used to recognize effort offers a handsome return on your investment of time and energy. This kind of return can have a powerful impact on any company, division, team, or individual. This success is felt throughout an organization as morale lifts, quality improves, production picks up, teams work more collaboratively, and organizational goals take precedence over personal agendas.

Production picks up because employees feel their ideas, suggestions, and concerns are being heard. People feel more secure about voicing complaints and making suggestions because they know management will focus on what is said, rather than who said it. People learn to see one another as valuable resources with whom they eagerly collaborate. In short, effort becomes more focused toward accomplishing the organization's business goals.

Consider the following ways that praise makes a real impact on an organization:

Ideas can result in cost savings, product improvement, and quality upgrades.

The Ford Motor Company and Toyota Motor Corporation have instituted programs that solicit employee suggestions. In one year, Ford received over 60,000 and Toyota received over 800,000 employee suggestions. As a result the companies benefitted from a wealth of new ideas. Employees felt their ideas were valued and knew their contribution had a direct impact on the business.

Days lost due to either illness or accident are reduced.

Disability claims are reduced, sick days are fewer, and motivation is higher. A greater sense of shared risk prevails because people understand what is involved to achieve the goal. They understand the importance of their sustained participation in that goal.

For example, Marianna Packing Company had over 700 accident-free days as a result of the effort of its employees. For every dollar spent on prevention, the company was saving $4 on premiums — a 300 percent savings.

When part of a prevention program, retraining and cross-training are faster, with a less severe learning curve. Also with such an effort, retention of key employees is higher and turnover is reduced throughout the organization.

Retention of employees is higher.

Ideo, a Palo Alto, California, product development company, has removed all job titles. They believe that the effort of one employee is as important as the effort of any other employee. Quality improves when people who have first-hand knowledge of a process are allowed and encouraged to apply that knowledge.

Herman Miller Company is ranked #456 of the Fortune 500. However, this small furniture manufacturing company has been an astonishing seventh in overall return to the investor for a period of over seven years. The company maintains this level by recognizing the efforts of employees. Anyone who contributes to the company's success with an idea that increases revenue (by itself or in conjunction with other ideas) is acknowledged with a percentage of the profits.

These examples spotlight how praise positively affects organizations and their stakeholders. They also show the variety of ways that praise can have a significant impact on an organization.

Now that it's clear how powerful praise really is, it's time to take a look at when praise does and does not work.

WHEN PRAISE WORKS

"I have yet to find the man, however exalted his station,
who did not do better work and put forth greater effort
under a spirit of approval than under a spirit of criticism."
— Charles Schwab, CEO, Charles Schwab & Co.

Praise works when it is used with —

- Enough frequency to signal others' awareness of effort
- Variety to indicate a sensitivity to the individual
- Value to target the uniqueness of each person
- The consequences in mind to focus our energies to better achieve positive goals

Here is a checklist to help you review your own praise-giving methods.

Remember that praise works when it is—

- Independent of other factors
- Specific
- Appropriate to the event or task
- Timely
- Delivered with sensitivity

WHEN PRAISE DOESN'T WORK

When important variables, such as an individual's efforts, diversity, styles, and degree of ownership of a task are ignored or undervalued, praise is no longer a tool, but merely a blunt instrument used to hack away at problems. The short-term consequence of this approach is one of general dissatisfaction. The long-term consequence is diminished effort and, carried to its ultimate consequence, business decline.

Here is a checklist to help you remember when praise does not work.

Praise fails when it is—

- A way to get others to feel indebted to you

- Given to only a select few

- Coupled with criticism, thereby diminishing the effectiveness of both the positive and the constructive comments

- Given to one individual at the expense of another

- Expressed in situations that would embarrass the recipient

- Offered so long after the praiseworthy event that its value is lost

- Used to enhance the position of the person offering it

FILTERS OF PRAISE

To truly understand when praise does and doesn't work, we need to examine the filters that affect the ways we give and receive praise. Life experiences filter the way we receive and transmit information. For example, the praise we experienced as a grade school student influenced how we expected, anticipated, or rejected praise opportunities as we went on in our schooling and, later, in our work. And when we gave praise, if our sincere attempts were met with sarcasm, embarrassment, or outright denial, those experiences undoubtedly began to filter how often we used praise and how much we valued it.

Such filtering can support or destroy the necessary foundation for a healthy praise experience. The focus those filters allow defines the way we see, hear, and experience various forms of recognition or praise.

Consider the following QUESTIONS as you review the praise filters that affect your own behavior.

How was praise used while you were growing up, both at home and at school?..

....

How was praise given when you attempted something? When you actually and successfuly completed something?...

....

In high school, did your primary social group use praise generously, selectively, or was it withheld altogether? How did the group offer praise?

....

Did one parent praise you differently than the other parent? How was it different?

....

Were you praised differently than a sibling of the other gender? How and when?

....

How were you praised compared to a sibling who was older or younger?

....

....

While growing up, what did you see or experience in the way friends' families used praise that differed from your own experience? ....

....

Did you see praise as either a reward or acknowledgement? ....

....

These filters affect us unconsciously, dramatically, and if we are not helped to be aware of them, permanently. When we acknowledge the filters, we are able to more objectively understand the basis for a particular reaction. We can then anticipate our own possible responses to praise and choose from a variety of praise-giving approaches that will be positively received.

Look at the EXAMPLES below to see the effects of some praise filters in action—

An eager new supervisor reported to his manager about an increase in productivity after implementing a change in the regular process. The manager acknowledged the supervisor's effort by sarcastically stating "Wow! How did we ever manage before you got here?" The supervisor, young and new to the work unit, was unsure if he were being positively recognized or if he were being told he was "too big for his britches."

An experienced employee was promoted to a new position and spoke with all the employees she would be managing to learn about them and their jobs. Each time she heard about a particular accomplishment or new idea, she was very specific in her interest, questions, and compliments. It confused her when she was met with indifferent and disbelieving responses. After some probing, she discovered that her employees' previous manager believed the only praise they needed or deserved as in the weekly pay envelope. The new manager wasn't sure what she had walked into with the new job.

Both of these examples show how the power of praise to motivate evaporated. Praise filters affected both the praise giving and receiving.

FOCUSING THE POWER OF PRAISE

Acknowledging effort is the focus of praise. The quality of that focus, whether it is sharp and targeted or broad and diffuse, determines how strongly it is felt, and how deeply it is respected.

In focusing the efforts of both the user and the receiver, praise serves as a tool. Much as we do with a laser beam of light, we focus on the desired aspect to be praised. The light beam narrows and targets specific people, events, and behaviors that deserve recognition. In both positive and negative situations, energy is needed to produce the desired end results, whether they include recognition of effort or of errors. While all events, positive and negative, need to be recognized, only those we want to continue should be praised.

Constructive criticism helps someone focus on what is not working effectively and how to apply another approach. Praise and criticism are two distinct tools and are not interchangeable. Each has distinctive timing, language, and clear-cut desired outcomes.

Whenever possible, praise and criticism should occur in two separate conversations. We often think we are softening the weight of a potentially negative statement by including a few positive comments. But when praise is given in the same conversation as criticism, the energy of one cancels out the other and the focus of praise is lost.

Example 1:

"This report is excellent, but it's three days late."

The focus of this statement rests on the second phrase, which lets the listener know that there is dissatisfaction. Because the choice of the word "excellent" is so general, and nothing is specific in the praise portion, the listener remembers the comment about the lateness of the report and experiences none of the positive focus.

Example 2:

"This report is late, but it's well-written."

This statement focuses on the praise portion, because the listener remembers you liked the report and that time didn't seem to be an issue for you. This well-intentioned, but ineffective, use of praise can send a message that its OK to produce work late, as long as the work is good. Mixed messages can come back to haunt the speaker and damage credibility.

Suggested Approach:
"You did an excellent job on the report. It's very well written. I'd like to give you the opportunity to do similar work in the future. And all of us know that deadlines are very important. We missed this one by several days. What suggestions do you have so we can provide quality reports within the time frames we have? (Asking people for their ideas is a way of valuing them.)

A FOCUSING ACTIVITY

For many people, separating praise from criticism is difficult. Time constraints, privacy issues, insufficient training, and a lack of clarity about the intent and desired outcomes all tend to deflect the focus of the energy needed to use this tool appropriately.

Think of a situation in which you received praise and criticism in the same conversation. **Describe the situation:**

What do you remember as the focus of the comments you were given?

....

....

What portion of the comments do you remember most specifically?

....

....

....

PRAISE IN THE WORKPLACE

Look at the following list of ways that we can praise others. Keep in mind that praise means recognizing someone's effort.

CHECK those techniques you personally use, or the ones you have experienced.

CIRCLE the numbers of those that are new to you and might be well received by your colleagues.

1. Invite a staff member or colleague to spend informal time with managers.

2. Provide the opportunity to learn a new skill to increase one's marketability.

3. Send a card thanking an employee for his/her overtime.

4. Display a banner when members of a team or task force consistently remove obstacles as they move toward a deadline.

5. Have a surprise lunch for the group before the completion of a project.

6. Give an occasional afternoon of release time when people have been working hard.

7. Invite employees to participate in cross-training as instructors of an area of special interest.

8. Give employees the opportunity to deliver a status report to a more senior level.

9. Award a title to an employee for dedicated, ongoing effort.

10. Put a laudatory letter in an employee's file for consistently good work.

A PRAISING ACTIVITY

The following brief scenario offers you an opportunity to give some thought to how you see praise an an effective tool in the workplace.

Assume you are the president of a brand new company. You have total control over budget and resource allocations, and strive for the highest standards in the industry for quality control, employee retention and high company morale.

Write out five ideas for different forms of praise you want to intitiate as part of the culture at your company. Ignore any preconceived ideas about how other companies look at cost, time, company culture, and resources...just work on ideas.

1.
....

....

2.
....

....

3.
....

....

4.
....

....

5.
....

....

THE
PRAISE
P R O C E S S

What really flatters a man is that you
think him worth the flattery.
—George Bernard Shaw

KEY POINTS

Three major elements make up the praise process. Praise givers need to identify opportunities; choose the best praise tool; and apply the best praise approach.

The praise process reinforces praiseworthy behavior through a variety of methods specific to each individual. After being praised, a person feels valued and works to have a positive impact on an organization.

Four building blocks of praise form the foundation of an effective praise process: timing/frequency, variety of approaches, with value apparent, and consequences recognized.

The praise process works in concert with the four building blocks of praise to creatively recognize individuals and their efforts in a manner that acknowledges and motivates.

DEFINING THE ELEMENTS OF PRAISE

The praise process is an effective means of introducing and implementing the skills necessary for using praise effectively. The main elements of the praise process help praise givers —

- Identify opportunities for using praise

- Choose the best tools in terms of words, timing, and sensitivity

- Consider a wide range of approaches with which to apply praise

- Create an environment in which individual effort is appreciated.

Using the praise elements helps praise givers —

Identify people who deserve praise.

The praise process helps to identify efforts that we may take for granted, ignore altogether, or assume are not valued by the person involved. Think about your co-worker who is always willing to pitch in and help without being asked. Do they ever feel taken for granted?

Choose tools of language, timing, and sensitivity that reflect a "praise-friendly" environment.

The praise process works with specific tools, such as choice of words, timing, and setting to ensure that people feel enhanced, rather than embarrassed by praise. Think about a supervisor who is easily embarrassed by public display, but who appreciates a sincere "Thank you."

Apply and use a wide variety of methods of praising.

The praise process encourages givers to use variety to recognize people as distinct individuals. Finding appropriate and meaningful ways acknowledge individual effort results in a workforce that is motivated and feels valued. Think about how people decorate their work space to reflect their own personalities. Praise should use the same attention to reflect the individual personalities of the receivers.

IMPLEMENTING THE PRAISE PROCESS ELEMENTS

In the following examples, you have three distinct situations to give you an opportunity to apply and practice the skills involved in using the praise process effectively. Read through each situation and decide what behavior need to be identified, how you'll recognize that behavior, and what alternatives you could consider to tailor your praise method appropriately.

Situation One

An employee who has been on the job for 15 months meets with you for a scheduled project update. Not only does she have all the project figures for you, but also a revised timeline, two suggestions to save on resources, and a summary of project progress that is so well written you can send it directly to your boss. The project is still weeks from completion, but you want to recognize this employee's contribution to making this project a continuing success.

Here is a chance to put each ELEMENT of the praise process into action—

1. Identify what behavior(s) and/or action(s) you want to praise. ....

....

....

....

....

2. Choose specific words that will let this employee know that you are aware of her extra efforts. Also let her know that you hope to see her self-motivation continued in her future work. ....

....

....

....

....

3. Apply two ways of acknowledging this employee. The first can be a verbal statement of appreciation. Be creative with the second method. Think of something that would be unexpected, but nonetheless appreciated, i.e.

a flower, a cartoon with a personal note, an invitation to sit in on a meeting that you know the person is interested in, or even homemade cookies for the person to share.

Statement: ....

....

....

....

Method: ....

....

....

....

Situation Two

Your boss is leaving on an important business trip in half an hour and has asked to sit in for a couple of minutes while your team gives its update on the new system going on-line next week. The update is almost concluded and your boss begins to move quietly toward the door. All of a sudden, one of your more vocal and assertive staff members decides that since the boss is available, it's a good time to air a pet peeve. The boss acknowledges the viewpoint and asks to schedule a time when the issue can be more fully discussed and receive his undivided attention.

Using the elements of the praise process, how would you acknowledge the way your boss handled this situation?

1. Identify what about your boss' behavior or action you want to acknowledge with praise. ....

....

....

....

....

2. Choose language that shows how the boss' behavior is of value and why it is appreciated. ....

....

....

....

....

3. Apply two ways to acknowledge the boss.

Statement: ....

....

....

....

Method: ....

....

....

....

Situation Three

You're having lunch with one of your colleagues who is talking about how tight company resources are right now and how unrelenting the workload demands are. You explain that you have two employees who have just finished a task and have actually expressed interest in the work of your colleague's group. You volunteer their services to your colleague, resulting in a win-win situation: the employees have a chance to learn new skills and your colleague has some additional help.

After arranging such a win-win situation, what would you like as praise from your colleague? From the employees? Use the praise process elements as a guideline.

From my colleague:

1. Identify what behavior or action of yours you want to have your colleague praise. ....

....

....

....

2. Choose the words you would like your colleague to use to let you know he/she is aware of your effort. ....

....

....

....

3. What method of praise would I appreciate having my colleague apply?

....

....

....

From the employees:

1. Identify what behavior or action of yours you want to have praised?

....

....

....

2. Choose the words you would like to hear. ....

....

....

3. What method of praise would I appreciate having my employee apply?

....

....

....

FOUR BUILDING BLOCKS OF PRAISE

Four building blocks of praise provide the foundation for a praise-healthy environment. They are timing or frequency, variety, value, and consequence.

- For praise to be valuable, it must be given often enough to establish it as part of the company culture.

- Praise is felt to be personal if it is varied; it should not be seen as simply a habitual response.

- The value of praise must be understood as a form of recognition that acknowledges and motivates, rather than simply rewards.

- When we praise people, we do so with consequences in mind so we consider the listener.

Let's take a closer look at each building block in greater detail.

Building Block One: TIMING/FREQUENCY

Praise is effective when it occurs often enough and close enough to the praiseworthy event, so people know their work is recognized. Praise, though, should not be given so often as to lose value.

Example: A man who had worked for one company for many years had just resigned and his colleagues were puzzled. He explained, "I guess I just got tired of never hearing anything good, except once a year when I had my review." Because he had brought in the most revenue and developed extraordinary relationships with his clients, he always received bonuses. However, he would have settled for something more personal and more often. The annual review recognized his successes, but did not frequently or even regularly acknowledge his efforts that were critical to those successes.

Building Block Two: VARIETY

In a praise-healthy environment, many approaches are used when recognizing effort so that the recognition never takes on a habitual feeling. Rote recognition means little.

Example: A woman who was the project lead on a company-wide initiative was asked how her efforts had been recognized when the project was successfully concluded. She answered, "Oh, I got the same shiny black rock everyone else did... I guess it was a paper weight, but most of us threw it away." Obviously, she felt her efforts deserved something specific and distinct from what others received. People need to be recognized for their individual efforts and contributions, not necessarily with more elaborate recognition, but certainly with recognition that is more personal. Taking time to find the particular variation most meaningful for the individual requires that the praise giver consider a wide variety of approaches to praise.

Building Block Three: VALUE

Praise is successful when it is specific and meaningful to the person or persons involved. The receiver really needs to know that the praise giver sees the individual as an important and effective contributor to the company's effort.

Example: "This project would never have been completed without you. We knew what we wanted, but you made it happen, maintained it and used imagination to even further develop it. Many thanks!" The team that received these words of praise was ecstatic with the recognition of the distinctive work they had done. Their work was unique and was valued as such by those who requested it, were involved with it, and those who benefited from it.

Building Block Four: CONSEQUENCES

A sensitive praise giver delivers a praise message carefully, anticipating in advance just what the results of that message may be.

Example: "As a customer service rep, I know that a good word can really motivate me. When I don't get one, I guess I'm more likely to take my frustration out on the customers. You know, those people who call in with the same questions I have to answer a hundred times every day. When I finally do get a kind word, I try to show it in my voice, and my level of patience. And, I have to admit, I try to give out more accurate information, as well!"

THESE
BUILDING BLOCK

OF PRAISE

PROVIDE
CLEAR GUIDELINES
FOR GIVING PRAISE BY:

1. Recognizing timing and frequency of efforts as soon as possible after they occur. By being aware of how often the desired effort takes place, you let others know, for example, when things are moving along on time and on budget, or when you receive particularly thoughtful proposals that go beyond boiler plate. You also clearly demonstrate an awareness and understanding of what is involved in doing their jobs.

2. Using a variety of approaches. Doing something slightly out of the ordinary to recognize the effort of others shows your willingness to stretch yourself for others. When you avoid doing things "the way they've always been done," you make a strong statement about seeing others as unique individuals.

3. Valuing the individual and recognizing that individual to be as unique as a fingerprint. You can tailor your praise with flowers for one person, a public announcement for another, and a personal handwritten note for a third. These all indicate that you see people as distinct individuals.

4. Being aware that the positive consequences of the ongoing use of carefully individualized praise are higher productivity, improved quality, lower turnover, reduced disability claims, less in-fighting, and fewer power vacuums.

APPLYING THE FOUR BUILDING BLOCKS OF PRAISE

Think of using the four building blocks by asking when they could be applied, what methods could be used, what reasons would be seen as appropriate, and what would happen if they weren't used.

From your own inventory of experiences, think of a situation that has improved after you praised the individuals involved. Jot down one or two ideas or phrases for each of the four building blocks that can apply.

First describe your situation ....

....

....

....

Timing/Frequency

How often do efforts that deserve recognition occur in my workplace? How frequently do I let the people involved know I am aware of their efforts? Do I acknowledge their contributions soon enough to have them value my praise? ....

....

....

....

Variety

What praise-giving methods are available to me so that I can recognize effort without falling into a predictable pattern and lessening the effect of the praise? ....

....

....

....

....

Value

In this situation what do I know about the person or team that will help me choose a method of praise that will be especially meaningful and relevant?

....

....

....

....

Consequence

What do I hope to have happen as a result of this recognition? In this specific situation, what might occur if this recognition isn't expressed?

....

....

....

....

....

REFLECTING ON THE BUILDING BLOCKS

Now review the building block information and answer the following questions:

1. Which building block is the most challenging for you to put into action in your workplace? ....

....

....

....

....

2. Which building block is the easiest for you to apply? ....

....

....

....

....

3. What specific consequences do you hope will result from your use of the building blocks? ....

....

....

....

....

RELATIONSHIP BETWEEN THE PRAISE PROCESS
AND THE FOUR BUILDING BLOCKS

The three elements of the praise process—in boldface—work together with the four building blocks—in italics.

1. *Identify the behavior that deserves to be recognized.*

2. **Think about how often this kind of behavior occurs.**

3. *Choose the best way of recognizing effort.*

4. **Think about the variety of ways to praise so the person feels unique.**

5. **Think about how a person who feels valued contributes positively to the organization.**

6. *Apply the use of praise.*

7. *Experience the positive benefits to the individual and the group when efforts are recognized and appreciated.*

SECTION THREE

PRAISE
AND COMMUNICATION

*Some fellows pay a compliment
like they expected a receipt.*
—Kin Hubbard

KEY POINTS

As a form of communication, praise conveys information about you, your work unit, and your company.

Body language conveys a message and makes a difference in the way a person "hears" praise.

Using praise requires that we learn to communicate differently.

Time spent communicating criticism far outweighs time spent communicating praise.

WHAT PRAISE COMMUNICATES
Information, Criticism (Blame), and Praise

As a form of communication, praise conveys information about you, your work unit, and your organization. Through your style, emphasis, and objectivity, people get a sense of how you use communication. The greatest percentage of communication in most workplaces usually involves a straight exchange of information: new procedures, meetings, upcoming projects. The second largest area of communication is usually devoted to constructive criticism, which is more often heard as blame. When something doesn't go smoothly, people talk about what happened, who did it and what the expected fallout will be. People often communicate as though the breakdown was the personal fault of an individual.

Because information exchange is impersonal and constructive criticism is often heard as blame, praise as a positive form of recognition seems all too remote to most people. Typical reasons for not giving praise:

- "I don't have time to pat them on the back—that's why they get a paycheck."

- "We work in two different cities, so they know if they don't hear from me, things are going OK."

- "They're a good team, and they all tell each other everyday how well they're doing."

Chart an average week's communication in your workplace. Estimate the percentage of conversation that makes up the simple exchange of information, constructive criticism, blame and praise.

Any Week at Work

PERCENTAGES:	EXCHANGE OF INFORMATION	CONSTRUCTIVE CRITICISM	BLAME	PRAISE
Your conversation with others:				
Your team members' conversations with each other:				
Your boss' conversation with you:				

OBSERVATIONS ON
PRAISE AND COMMUNICATION

The universal challenge with either giving or receiving praise is communicating the message effectively. How we recognize and offer approval to others and how graciously we are able to accept praise that is given to us is tied to our communication skills. The presence or the absence of praise in a work environment signals important information about the organization. One of the most frequent comments about the lack of praise is that it takes too much time. People feel pressured and constrained just to meet the daily demands of their own jobs. When asked to think carefully and plan to use the added skill of praise consciously, they often feel overwhelmed.

Take the case of Jake who works for a company making packaging for the semiconductor industry. Jake, an operations manager, has been with this corporation for 12 years. He is regarded as tough, thorough, and fair. He has just received a new addition to his staff, Ken, who seems very eager. Jake has spoken with Ken a couple of times, very informally, letting him know when his work has seemed a little off track and how he'd like Ken to make some changes.

Jake feels it's useful to keep all his people in the information loop because it's important for them to have a sense of the organization's direction and what role their own division plays in that move. But Jake also feels people know when something is working, so he shouldn't have to take the time to "pat them on the head," as he calls it.

One morning Jake arrived to find Ken had caught up on all the past-due orders. He had also planned out the schedule for the next two weeks to clear up some shipping backlogs. As Ken came in, Jake smiled and said, "I see you've finally got those past-dues straightened out!"

Ken was livid. All his time and energy and never a word of praise! In fact, the little acknowledgement Ken *does* receive comes across as criticism. Frustrated, Ken talks with a friend outside of work and says, "It seems like 90 percent of what my boss talks about is how to do the job, when to do it, and what we need to get it done on time. The rest of the time Jake tells me what he doesn't like or what isn't working. I never hear a good word from him."

Telling people their efforts are appreciated is not a simple task, nor is it one for which the intent should be taken for granted. The better our skills are in communicating both the awareness of and appreciation for a person's efforts, the greater the likelihood we will be accurately heard. Effectively communicating praise, in turn, will lead to reinforcing those behaviors that earn praise.

Few of us are aware of what percentage of our communication is devoted to praise, as opposed to exchange of information or constructive criticism. All too often, communication seems more heavily weighted on criticism or giving direction than on the proverbial pat on the back.

In your workplace, do you feel that the amounts of praise versus information and criticism break down into the percentages shown in this graphic? If so, a review of what your praise efforts actually communicate will help increase your praise percentage.

Any Day at Work

Source: Author's Experience

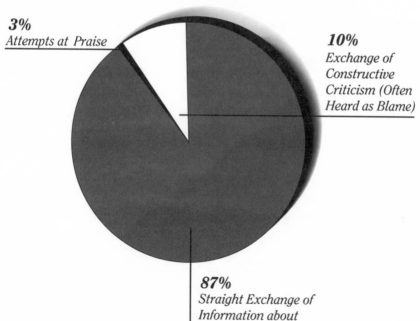

3%
Attempts at Praise

10%
Exchange of Constructive Criticism (Often Heard as Blame)

87%
Straight Exchange of Information about How to Get the Job Done

HOW PRAISE IS STATED:
Always consider the listener

When acknowledging someone's effort, the praise giver must choose the right words, determine the proper time, and be aware of the listener's point of view. Think of your own reactions, especially when being praised. Why is it so difficult for us to hear the words that applaud our efforts? When people choose not to hear praise, the likelihood of being praised in the future is reduced. When praise isn't accepted, people get it less and less frequently and then complain that they aren't appreciated. But let's look at the positive side of communicating praise. If the praise process is used correctly, the listener will hear the praise loud and clear. Consider the following examples, and ask yourself about the differences in each pair:

1. "Your work is good, keep it up."
   vs.
   "Your work reflects a lot of time and thought. You obviously researched the topic thoroughly and the finished report shows it!"

2. "It's great to have you at this seminar."
   vs.
   "I'm glad you came. There are several people who would like to meet you."

3. "Your team is super."
   vs.
   "Your team really works collaboratively. It's obvious that they discuss options and try for workable alternatives everyone can live with."

4. "This project was a snap."
   vs.
   "This project came in on time and under budget."

What is wrong with the praise statements? How are the listeners affected by each?

1. ....

2. ....

3. ....

4. ....

SAY IT, HEAR IT, SEE IT

It is not uncommon to hear a person speak and walk away without the listeners being able to repeat a word—even though they know intuitively what was *meant* simply by reading the speaker's body language. When praise is expressed publicly or privately, the praise giver's body language, or non-verbal communication, makes as big an impact on the listener as the message itself. It's easy to forget that what you as a praise giver mean may not be the same as what your listeners hear.

Look at the examples below. Think about your own cultural and personal biases as you write your impression of the message that's being sent or suggested:

Example 1:

Tom the production line manager, is getting ready to announce Total Quality Management (TQM) awards at a quarterly meeting. As he steps up to the microphone to introduce the recipients, his shoulders slump and he speaks in a monotone. Staring at his notes, never looking up, Tom seems to sigh after reading each name.

From Tom's body language, I can assume: ....

....

....

....

Commentary:

From Tom's body language, the recipients might make several different assumptions that could influence how readily they accept the TQM award and what they see as the level of Tom's sincerity.

Some might assume Tom is not interested, or haughty, or perhaps even feeling inconvenienced by having to participate in this quarterly meeting. For the people receiving the awards, Tom's behavior might take a lot of the pleasure out of the event.

Tom's sighs, his posture, and even his vocal monotone could easily convey someone who has things other than employee recognition on his mind. His attitude might make the reward recipient feel intrusive or unimportant. The real reason might be that Tom feels uncomfortable speaking to a large group.

Whenever praise is offered, it is an extension of the person giving it. If that person sends mixed messages about the value of the praise, it's value is lessened.

Example 2:

Anna had been cross-training a new supervisor who was having a hard time grasping some of the policies and procedures of the work unit. It now looks like Anna's persistence finally paid off as the new supervisor describes how she was able to follow one of the complex procedures from start to finish. Anna listens to the supervisor and then rolls her eyes skyward. She clasps her hands in an attitude of prayer.

From Anna's body language, I can assume: ....

....

....

....

Commentary:

It might be reasonable to assume Anna was totally unprofessional, rolling her eyes, and making what might be seen by some as inappropriate gestures. What we need to consider is Anna herself. Is it possible that there are different cultural dynamics at work between Anna and the new supervisor? How dramatic is that difference? Some cultures are more demonstrative than others. In some groups, physical expression is considered not only appropriate, but it is anticipated.

Another view of Anna's behavior might suggest that her acknowledgement of the employee's efforts suggests humor. If that is the case, the humor could be seen as good-natured, but might also be interpreted as sarcastic.

If Anna is really appreciative of her employee's perseverance and she is being sincere, she needs to consider how the employee might read her behavior. Should Anna assume that the employee understands what she is trying to convey?

Example 3:

You've been called into the office of the senior v-p. Your most recent project is the topic, and the senior v-p is clear and emphatic about how your insightful handling saved money and used resources very effectively. You and the senior v-p both stand up and hands are extended for a congratulatory shake when all of a sudden you find yourself in a bear hug.

From the senior v-p's body language, I can assume: ....

....

....

....

....

Commentary:

The senior v-p's behavior can lead to a great many different assumptions. The first might be unbridled, spontaneous pleasure at how effectively you handled the project.

A second and more volatile assumption might be that the behavior is a sexual advance (gender notwithstanding). This interpretation can lead to harassment charges and defeat what might have been sincerely intended as praise.

A third assumption about the behavior is similar to the situation with Anna, where cultural differences are being experienced. (I've been hugged by clients myself, so I see it as enthusiasm, appreciation, and sometimes it's even been relief on their part that a problem has been resolved.)

✳✳✳✳

These three examples of praise situations focus on some interpretations that happen all too frequently. People who are well-intentioned, and who want to let others know that their efforts have been noted, may be unaware of the effect they have on others. When the building blocks and praise process are not used conscientiously, the person deserving of praise may not get the intended message. For both the giver and the receiver, the praise should be communicating the same message.

PRAISING STYLES

If you aren't comfortable communicating your praise to others, it's unlikely others will be comfortable hearing it. If we aren't used to being praised, we feel an initial awkwardness that we express in behaviors, attitudes, and expressions. Read through the praising styles described below and see if one or more might apply to someone you know.

Throwaway:
"Yeah, it was really great that you made the deadline, and I know we'll keep moving forward. I've got to run to my next meeting. Maybe we can talk about this again. Keep up the great work!"

Jokester:
"No kidding, we didn't think someone with such a tiny voice would ever be able to stand up in front of the important people of our company and talk!"

Martyr:
"I'm glad you're doing so well on the project. I took myself off because I knew how important it was to you and it's good to see you accomplishing what I'd planned."

Embarrassed:
"Well, uh, ah, it's good that you know, you did, the uh, good job on the download. We really needed it and you, gosh, you really came through for everyone. I don't know what to say."

Exercise: Using the praising style examples, please answer the following questions:

Was the person benefiting from the praise easily identified?

Throw Away	Yes__	No__
Martyr	Yes__	No__
Jokester	Yes__	No__
Embarrassed	Yes__	No__

Did the choice of language reflect a work environment that used praise effectively?

Throw Away	Yes__	No__
Martyr	Yes__	No__
Jokester	Yes__	No__
Embarrassed	Yes__	No__

Was it clear how often the behavior occured and how frequently that behavior was praised?

Throw Away	Yes__	No__
Martyr	Yes__	No__
Jokester	Yes__	No__
Embarrassed	Yes__	No__

Did the value of the praise and the related consequence of not offering it appear clear?

Throw Away	Yes__	No__
Martyr	Yes__	No__
Jokester	Yes__	No__
Embarrassed	Yes__	No__

The praise process can help you identify what deserves praise. Choose the words, behaviors, or activities to convey what is valued, and take the time to apply this process. It benefits not only the person who receives praise, but also the person who practices these skills, and ultimately, everyone involved.

USING THE BUILDING BLOCKS
AND THE PRAISE PROCESS TO COMMUNICATE

Using the building blocks and the praise process is essential for building a foundation for a praise-healthy environment, and for developing your own styles of praising effectively. Being aware of the timing and frequency with which praise is given, expanding your variety of praise approaches, knowing what will be of value to the recipient and keeping consequences in mind, people will begin to create an environment where individuals appreciate one another, and express that appreciation openly.

DEVELOPING NEW COMMUNICATION SKILLS

Given all the choices for misinterpretation, how can you convey to others the kinds of praise that are most personally meaningful? What are the acceptable forms for letting the people you work with know what has meaning for you? Do you want to be offered a company title, your own parking space, participation in strategy meetings, etc.? How do you let others know what will motivate you?

Here are questions you might ask people at work. They indicate on a practical level that praise is significant and meaningul to you in your workplace.

YOUR BOSS:
How can recognition for good service be built into my performance plan?
How can a specific form of recognition be part of the perks offered through the company?

Your Own Specific Question:

....

....

YOUR COLLEAGUES:
If the corporate culture could support a friendly competition that includes choosing your own rewards, what might some of those rewards be?
How does the cross-functional team generate and agree to various forms of preferred praise at the start of a task?

Your Own Specific Question:

....

....

YOUR REPORTING STAFF:
How can open communication be established where the topic of praise is discussed as it applies to all members of the work group?
How can a method be devised to recognize individual contributions without undermining the morale of other team members?

Your Own Specific Question:..

....

....

PRACTICING NEW SKILLS

Developing or expanding the skill of communicating praise requires practice. From your own experience in the workplace, choose a situation that you feel deserves your recognition.

Your situation:

....

....

....

By first developing and then practicing responses to each of the three situations listed below, you have an opportunity to clearly identify what you want to acknowledge. You can use this practice opportunity to learn more about how effectively you use the building blocks of praise. Choose the words that will exactly convey your awareness of the effort put into the task, and then decide on the praise setting that will be most satisfying to the person involved.

Briefly describe the current situation involving the need for communicating praise in your own workplace. Then write a sentence for each of the following; use the examples to help you get started.

1. You are aware and appreciative of an individual's effort.
    (Example: "Jane, you've been putting in a lot of time on your own. I really appreciate your professionalism and follow-through.") ....

....

2. You wish to focus specifically on what was done well.
    (Example: "Your efforts are responsible for this project's getting completed on time. It's making a valuable difference in the attitude of the others on the team and with our client who gave us this tight schedule." ....

....

3. You have decided to praise the individual in the way most comfortable for that person.
    (Example: "I know you don't like a big fuss, so I' didn't announce this at the staff meeting. But it really deserves a special thanks, so I am putting a letter of commendation in your personnel file and I have a copy here for you to read.")
    ....

....

SECTION FOUR

MOVING THE COMPANY TOWARDS A

P R A I S E

FRIENDLY ENVIRONMENT

Great minds discuss ideas,
average minds discuss events,
small minds discuss people.
—Admiral Hyman G. Rickover

KEY POINTS

The changing workplace creates the need for greater varieties of praise.

Every organization has its own praise process.

Whatever praise tools your company currently uses can benefit from adopting, adapting, combining, and modifying additional ways of praising.

When people value the praise they receive, it reflects an orgainizational environment sensitive to each individual.

THE CHANGING WORKPLACE, WORK AND WORKER

In recent years the workplace has undergone dramatic changes. As a result, employees may feel that what was once a supportive environment is no longer quite so inviting. People in the present-day workplace are expected to be grateful that they have jobs.

Given this situation, is it realistic to expect workers to see work as its own reward when conditions have changed dramatically in three specific areas: the workplace, the work and the worker?

Historically, the workplace was a factory line, a counter, an office. Today it is a cubicle, a modem, or even the car phone. While this change shows responsiveness to the need for flexibility, often it creates a sense of isolation; direct response to feedback is difficult, creating feelings that risks are not shared.

The work itself has changed. Most workers used to produce something. Now employees are involved in a process, project, or service. In such a setting, it is more difficult to feel essential. Instead there's a lack of an overall sense of contribution. Giving praise in a work environment where people don't feel involved or vital is much more difficult. Recognition may taper off entirely.

Once the worker was seen as the backbone of an organization, loyal, committed. Now employees are often seen as self-interested, even a hindrance because of having such narrowly defined skills, or because of needing training. The company, once seen as a surrogate family to be given unlimited loyalty, is now seen as a hard-to-please parent.

So, the workplace, the work itself, and the worker have all undergone tremendous changes. These changes have made it difficult to believe in the sincerity of praise, especially when it is such a rare occurrence in many work environments.

Today's workplace needs people who feel valued. As business continues to move forward into this ever-expanding world of technology, how we treat people and how we recognize their contributions will determine how successful we really are.

THE COMPANY'S PERSPECTIVE ON PRAISE

Valuing individuals for who they are and what they do suggests an appreciation for the unique effort of each person. Valued workers on an assembly line will help the board of directors of a company achieve a greater profit margin than those employees who are taken for granted.

In healthy organizations—those that are truly praise-friendly environments—recognition and approval move in all directions and come in many forms. Everyone rewards, reinforces, and rekindles the spark which distinguishes between neglect and value.

"The difference between a flower girl and a lady is not how they act, but rather how they're treated." This line from *My Fair Lady* points out that the difference between a valued employee and a neglected employee is as simple as how we acknowledge one another.

Organizations may vary in their approaches to praise. Some support very public and frequent recognition, while others have a lower-key praising style. Other companies may ignore praise altogether. The subtle, often unspoken corporate culture influences how people give and receive praise and the manner in which praise is expressed.

Think about the kinds of PRAISE your company supports.

Here are some examples of positive feedback.

- Customer service representatives receive a balloon bouquet in recognition of favorable customer feedback.
- New employees choose their own titles for their business cards.
- Project teams have lunch courtesy of the company once a month regardless of what's going on with the project.
- Surprise pizza arrives when people are putting in long hours.

Another idea that would work in your situation:

-

....

....

RATE YOUR COMPANY'S PRAISE ENVIRONMENT

Consider each of the following statements. Determine whether the statement is true or false for your specific organization:

T   F   1. Praise is encouraged throughout the company at all levels.

T   F   2. Senior management models the use of praise effectively and consistently.

T   F   3. Employees understand that their efforts are recognized when they are praised.

T   F   4. It is most appropriate for mid- and senior-level people to praise only those who report directly to them.

T   F   5. Praising one's boss is asking for problems with your own peers.

T   F   6. It is appropriate to express appreciation only in public groups where nothing can be misunderstood.

T   F   7. Praise is private and personal and good taste demands that it not be done publicly.

T   F   8. When one member of a team or task force is praised, all members of the same group should be equally praised.

T   F   9. Most people are too embarrassed to accept praise.

T   F   10. Praise is offered in the midst of a long project, not only when that project is completed.

A HEALTHY COMPANY'S PRAISE ENVIRONMENT

A company that offers frequent, valuable recognition to its employees at all levels has a praise-healthy work environment. If an organization uses the praise building blocks and the praise process as a regular part of the work day, that company respects and values each employee as a unique contributor to the success of the whole organization. Taking the pulse of such a praise-healthy company will show the following vital signs:

1. Evidence of praise at all levels reflects a healthy work environment where employees from the CEO to the receptionist recognize the value of praise.

2. Senior management's positive behavior with regard to praise affects the entire company. The frequency and effectiveness that people across all company lines use to recognize each other's efforts make praise an effective tool.

3. The workplace is a praise-friendly environment where recognition of effort is fundamental to achieving success.

4. Praise to and from direct reports is always considered appropriate behavior. From the CEO to the cafeteria worker, the inventory clerk to the manager of information systems, all employees demonstrate an awareness of, and an appreciation for, the efforts of others.

5. Senior people are less likely to be the recipients of praise. In a healthy company, everyone who deserves recognition receives it.

6. Though public recognition is valuable to some, and intimidating to others, in a healthy company the most effective praise considers the individual receiving it and what makes him/her most comfortable.

7. Praise acknowledges effort that can be individual or group-related. Praise given in a specific and timely manner, with genuine appreciation, motivates people to better levels of work.

8. If we as employees are concerned that our comments won't be heard, we will never offer them. It's important to praise people for taking the risk to offer suggestions for new methods, services, or products. Appropriate praise for such worker motivation helps ensure a vital and progressive company.

TAKE YOUR COMPANY'S PRAISE PULSE

Now, think about three to five of the most prevalent expressions of praise that are used in your company, division, or team: ....

....

....

....

On the basis of your knowledge of your fellow workers, what might be the most meaningful form of praise you could use with them? ....

....

....

....

Describe any behavior or language that is currently used to praise in your workplace. In your opinion are either the praising words or actions inappropriate or unappreciated? ....

....

....

What expression of praise would have greatest value for you, personally?

....

....

From your boss: ....

....

From your colleagues: ....

....

From your reporting staff: ....

....

....

BUILDING BETTER COMPANIES
Some Ideas to Consider

Companies that have found their own unique methods to recognize effort and praise their employees have found the results gratifying and rewarding. The following examples are intended to give you ideas that you can try out, modify, or combine in your own organization:

Method	The CEO takes 10-15 calls a week from employees. These are not from his direct reports, but rather from employees at all levels of the company, who call with complaints, suggestions, requests, and ideas. Whenever possible, the CEO acts on the ideas himself.
Result	Employees know they are valued and they know the CEO has an awareness of the issues they face.
Method	A expanding company needed a new facility. Every employee was given the authority to configure his own workspace.
Result	A space that is designed with professional and personal efficiency as well as comfort in mind contributes to higher productivity and increased quality.
Method	One software company encourages its employees to create their own titles on business cards. Some read Resident Wizard, Organizer of Space, and Budget Beast.
Result	Employees feel a strong sense of ownership of their job, and bring humor to the workplace, improving morale and increasing performance.

Method	Every day a company provides free hot lunches prepared by a gourmet chef for all employees. The chef also prepares box dinners for the engineers every evening.
Result	Employees save time and are more productive, as they stay on site. They know they have a valuable benefit.

Method	Each employee receives a glass bowl filled with marbles from the company. The marbles are distinctive in size, shape, and color for each employee. Anyone, at any time, at any level of the organization can place one of their marbles in another's bowl. Anyone seeing another's bowl can tell that one person has recognized the effort of another.
Result	This method encourages praise across all lines at the company because even the CEO has a bowl of marbles. The company even refers to the marbles in performance reviews, noting who has given out marbles and who needs to be coached in the value of praising others.

No matter what the praise method, as long as it is valued by the receiver, the effort reinforces itself and reflects a work environment sensitive to individuals. Praise provides dividends in clearer communication, better work output, and a stronger commitment to the organization—if people know they are valued.

I n reviewing the critical concepts of praise, we all know that people like to feel recognized. We all enjoy receiving approval in a variety of forms and need to understand that praise is a tool available to anyone.

- Praise is available to CEOs and systems analysts, to sales people and secretaries, to brokers, bankers, and bartenders.

- Praise recognizes effort, a validation that must occur if success is ever to follow. Effort is something often dismissed until it results in what is seen as success. Without effort, there would never be success.

In a recent conversation, a young man remarked on the lack of polish in a concert performance. His friend said, "I know what you mean, but I respect the effort it took to get up there and try." In the workplace, we all must get up and try. This produces possibilities and solutions, rather than perpetuating problems and becoming subject to them.

It is important to take the initiative, accept praise risks, and support your co-workers who do likewise. When evaluating a project that has gone off track in time and budget, don't spend time looking for someone to blame. It may be more useful to find out what—rather than *who*—went wrong. That action is deserving of praise. Taking a chance means not always saying or doing popular things. Companies give lip service to the idea of risk taking but often punish those who do so and don't win every time.

Note the last time you took a risky chance to OFFER praise.

What did you do or say? ....

....

....

....

When will you take your next chance? And how will you convey your praise? ....

....

....

....

So, why is praise such a rare commodity in today's workplace? *Perhaps people don't praise because they are uninformed about what others do and so don't know what to say.* Perhaps this lack of information is due to time constraints, the awkwardness of various situations, or the isolation of the workplace. Whatever the reason, the lack of praise, or even worse, praise that is so generic it has no value to the receiver, sends a message to all employees and they know whether they are valued or neglected.

How do we turn this situation around? Almost every group has staff meetings, project meetings, manager meetings, etc.

- Try to use the first five minutes of regularly scheduled meetings for people to identify the most significant accomplishment of the past week.

- Try to allocate a space on a common bulletin board for a monthly notice of positive efforts and how those efforts support long term goals.

- Try to use the department newsletter to recognize effort and explain how that effort is valuable.

Another Idea: ....

....

....

....

....

....

Another reason for the rarity of praise has to do with a prevalent attitude that says, "You get a salary, what else do you need?" With job scarcity, many companies feel employees should realize they are lucky to be employed. Employees themselves have come to rarely expect recognition. They may hope for it, but when praise is forthcoming, it is always a surprise and for some, a treasured gift.

- Try to write a letter and get several co-workers to sign it. It takes only about five minutes and a piece of paper. You could indicate one thing each of you has benefitted from as a result of your contact with the colleague who is receiving the letter. Make a copy and frame it, or give it to the manager to present. Such a visible sign will let management know that what employees are doing is appreciated in this praise-friendly environment.

Another Idea: ....

....

....

....

....

Praise has a short and erratic life span in the workplace due to the emphasis placed on the stockholder, to the exclusion of those who make the returns to the stockholder possible. Look at a company's mission statements that have stockholders, customers and employees listed in that order. When the hierarchy is stacked this way, it conveys volumes about who is valued, who is important and about who receives rewards.

Who comes first in your company? What should the order be, in your opinion? In some of the world's most successful companies, employees are mentioned first, then customers and finally stockholders. It's simple. If the employee doesn't receive approval, the quality, productivity, and loyalty are going to be affected and when the customers suffer, so do the stockholders.

Another Idea:..

....

....

....

....

Lastly, instability may be thought of as a reason praise isn't more prevalent in the workplace today. Many people believe that instability is a way of life and people should just get used to it and get on with things. There isn't any strong disagreement with that and at the same time, it doesn't mean people should be neglected.

Use the instability of the workplace as the reason, the motivation for continued conversation with people about what is going well, how people can be of help to one another and how appreciative human beings are when they are treated graciously.

Praise needs to travel in all directions. The more it is used, the more it will come back to those who have used it. A powerful story is about a manager and her senior analyst. The senior analyst had been put in charge of an enormous, highly visible task. Despite the manager's nervousness, the analyst successfully designed and implemented the task, resulting in kudos for the manager. For the manager, the most important praise came, not from her manager, but from the analyst who, over lunch one day, handed her a card. The card thanked the manger for what was seen as an opportunity, and for "running interference for me so I could get my work done." The manager later learned that the analyst had also gone to the manager's senior v-p to thank him for the wonderful support the manager had provided. None of this involved much time or expense. The benefit to everyone involved, however, was apparent both in savings of time and money, and enhanced credibility for the analyst and the manager.

Without the daily effort, there will be no big successes.

- Big success follows the small day to day effort, without which there will be no big successes.
- Big success follows the small day to day efforts with praise as the catalyst. Day to day effort deserves the thanks, the time and the respect of everyone.

Thank You

CHARACTERISTICS OF PRAISE WELL GIVEN

Provides recognition in a timely manner. Saving the 'good news' for the next performance review or for a big meeting scheduled two weeks away gives the appearance that convenience matters more than the recipient.

Recognizes that all people are unique contributors and acknowledges their individual contributions.

Avoids assumptions. The praise giver takes the time to learn something about the person being praised so that the methods will be valued by him or her.

Instills recognition as a part of the work culture. When people know they are recognized and their work appreciated, they tend to be more productive, give greater attention to quality, and generate more creative approaches to problems and processes.

States the recognition with sincerity. Those who offer praise because they "have to" or because they "are supposed to" diminish the value of the praise as well as their own credibility as leaders.

Establishes a level of trust among the receivers of praise. Employees learn and believe that what they do makes a difference to the health of the company as a whole. They understand that there are "good" consequences at the workplace and that they can directly influence the growth of a team, a project or the company.